Published by Creative Education
and Creative Paperbacks
P.O. Box 227, Mankato, Minnesota 56002
Creative Education and Creative Paperbacks
are imprints of The Creative Company
www.thecreativecompany.us

Design by The Design Lab
Production by Joe Kahnke
Art direction by Rita Marshall
Printed in the United States of America

Photographs by Alamy (Mark Conlin, Leonid
Serebrennikov), Corbis (Christophe Courteau/Water
Rights, Jeffrey L. Rotman), Dreamstime (Yap Kee Chan,
Julia Freeman-Woolpert, Piccaya, Kseniya Ragozina,
Oleg Sidashin, Sergey Uryadnikov, Wisiel), Flickr (Bill
Bumgarner), Shutterstock (indigolotos, Beverly Speed)

Library of Congress Cataloging-in-Publication Data
Bodden, Valerie.
Crabs / Valerie Bodden.
p. cm. — (Amazing animals)
Summary: A basic exploration of the appearance, be-
havior, and habitat of crabs, the widespread shelled
crustaceans. Also included is a story from folklore ex-
plaining why crabs look as though they are headless.
Includes bibliographical references and index.
ISBN 978-1-60818-752-2 (hardcover)
ISBN 978-1-62832-360-3 (pbk)
ISBN 978-1-56660-794-0 (eBook)
1. Crabs—Juvenile literature.
QL444.M33 B683 2017
595.3/86—dc23   2016004785

CCSS: RI.1.1, 2, 4, 5, 6, 7; RI.2.2, 5, 6, 7, 10;
RI.3.1, 5, 7, 8; RF.1.1, 3, 4; RF.2.3, 4

First Edition HC 9 8 7 6 5 4 3 2 1
First Edition PBK 9 8 7 6 5 4 3 2 1

AMAZING ANIMALS

CRABS

BY VALERIE BODDEN

CREATIVE EDUCATION • CREATIVE PAPERBACKS

Crabs are crustaceans (*kruh-STA-shuns*). Crustaceans have a hard shell and live in water. There are more than 6,700 different kinds of true crabs in the world!

Graceful rock crabs live in the Pacific Ocean

A crab's flat body is covered by a shell called a carapace

A crab's shell covers its wide, flat body. Crabs have 10 legs. The first two legs have claws for grabbing **prey**. Some crabs are brown or gray. Others are bright colors like blue, red, or yellow.

prey animals that are killed and eaten by other animals

The tiniest crabs are as small as spiders. But the biggest crabs have bodies the size of footballs. Their legs can stretch more than 12 feet (3.7 m) from tip to tip! They can weigh up to 40 pounds (18.1 kg).

The Japanese spider crab is the largest crab in the world

*Harlequin crabs (opposite)
live inside sea cucumbers,
animals on the ocean floor*

Most crabs live in the **ocean**.
Some live in deep, cold waters. Others
live along warm beaches. Some kinds of
crabs live in rivers. Others live on land.

ocean a big area of deep, salty water

Sally Lightfoot crabs use the ends of their claws like fingers to eat fish

Crabs will eat almost anything. Their favorite foods are **mussels**, snails, fish, worms, and **insects**. Some crabs eat seaweed, fruits, or leaves, too.

insects small animals with three body parts and six legs

mussels animals that live in the water and have a double shell

*A female crab's eggs
look like a big sponge
beneath her body*

A female crab lays thousands or millions of eggs. The eggs hatch as legless **larvae**. The larvae grow and shed their shells. They grow bigger shells. After shedding many times, they grow legs. Now they look like adult crabs. Some crabs live only a few years. But the biggest crabs can live up to 100 years!

larvae the form some animals take when they hatch from eggs, before changing into their adult form

Crabs usually walk sideways. They can walk on land or on the seafloor. Crabs that spend a lot of time on land can run fast. Some kinds of crabs are good swimmers, too.

Crab legs bend outward, so this makes them walk sideways

A hole on a beach (left) or underwater (opposite) makes a safe spot

Crabs hide from **predators** to stay safe. Most crabs dig a hole in sand or mud to hide. But some crabs hide by covering their shells with seaweed, **sponges,** or pieces of wood.

predators animals that kill and eat other animals

sponges sea animals with many holes in their skeleton

Some people keep crabs as pets. Others see crabs in the wild on beaches or in zoos. These sidestepping animals are always fun to watch!

A small crab might sneak under a person's hat at the beach

A Crab Story

Why do crabs look like they have no head? People in Africa told a story about this. They said a creator made all animals. She made Crab's body but told him to come back the next day for his head. Crab bragged that he was going to have the best head. This made the creator mad. She said Crab would not have a head at all.

Read More

Herriges, Ann. *Crabs*. Minneapolis: Bellwether Media, 2007.

West, David. *Tide Pool Animals*. North Mankato, Minn.: Smart Apple Media, 2014.

Websites

Enchanted Learning: Crabs
http://www.enchantedlearning.com/subjects/Crab.shtml
This site has crab facts and a picture to print and color.

San Diego Zoo Kids: Coconut Crab
http://kids.sandiegozoo.org/animals/arthropods/coconut-crab
Learn more about coconut crabs.

Note: Every effort has been made to ensure that the websites listed above are suitable for children, that they have educational value, and that they contain no inappropriate material. However, because of the nature of the Internet, it is impossible to guarantee that these sites will remain active indefinitely or that their contents will not be altered.

Index